— THE —
APPLE
COOKBOOK

Varieties text written by
Joan Morgan

THE
APPLE
COOKBOOK

EDITED BY
NICOLA HILL

Mitchell Beazley

First published in Great Britain in 1994
by Mitchell Beazley
an imprint of Reed Consumer Books Limited
Michelin House, 81 Fulham Road, London SW3 6RB
and Auckland, Melbourne, Singapore and Toronto

ISBN 1 85732 412 9

A CIP catalogue record for this book is available from
the British Library

Printed in Singapore

Acknowledgements

Art Director: Jacqui Small
Art Editors: Meryl James & Sue Michniewicz
Commissioning Editor: Nicola Hill
Editors: Isobel Holland & Jo Lethaby
Production Controller: Sasha Judelson
Photographer: Nick Carman
Home Economist: Jennie Shapter
Stylist: Jane McLeish
Illustrator: Marc Adams

Notes

Both metric and imperial measurements have been
given in all recipes. Use one set of measurements only
and not a mixture of both.

Standard level spoon measurements are used in all
recipes.
1 tablespoon = one 15 ml spoon
1 teaspoon = one 5 ml spoon

Eggs should be size 3 unless otherwise stated.

Milk should be full fat unless otherwise stated.

Ovens should be preheated to the specified temperature
– if using a fan assisted oven, follow the manufacturer's
instructions for adjusting the time and the temperature.

Variety notes – include appearance to give a very
general guide to its identity; texture and flavour; and
when appropriate cooking properties.

Availability – indicates the country and the time of
year when this variety appears on sale. (NB only
Britain, Europe and North America are given)

Storage – At home, apples should be stored in cool
conditions and preferably in the dark. Centrally heated
rooms or warm kitchens are not good places to keep
fruit, even if you intend to eat it fairly quickly. Fruit
that you want to store for any length of time and buy
from, for example, a farm shop to give a winter supply
will need to be kept in a shed, cellar or larder in which
a fairly low temperature can be maintained. It should
be frost-proof, reasonably well ventilated and care
should be taken to ensure that mice cannot get in and
also that no volatile chemicals or root vegetables are
stored close by, as fruit will readily become tainted and
pick up the smell of say, paraffin or onions.

The apple is the most versatile of all our fruits. From apple soup to apple sauce, a myriad of apple puddings and the finale of a fresh fruit dessert, there are an infinite number of ways to enjoy this delectable fruit. Apple juice is one of the most refreshing of all fruit drinks and apples can be turned into cider and cider brandy. The apple's versatility lies not only in its wide range of flavours, textures and colours but also in its ability to be used for both savoury and sweet dishes. Apples can compliment rich meats such as pork and goose, enhance vegetable salads, yet also make delicious fruit pies and tarts.

Most of the varieties on sale are primarily eating apples, but many may also be cooked and are regarded as dual purpose. Britain, however, continues to draw a firm distinction between dessert and culinary varieties. This derives from the Victorian era, when all apples were categorized into those of the finest eating quality, which were destined for the fresh fruit dessert, and cooking apples, which were large, very acidic and too sharp ever to be eaten fresh.

Dual purpose and eating varieties, on the other hand, have much less acidity and tend to retain their shape during cooking, a property that fits them for recipes such as *Tarte aux Pommes* or *tarte Tatin*, but their taste is sweet and mild by comparison with a traditional English cooker.

Modern storage has tended to erode the notion of season but, if fruit is kept at home, the dual purpose varieties are best used for cooking early in their season, when they have their maximum acidity and then after storing and mellowing they can be eaten fresh when the flesh is sweeter.

Early season varieties ripening in the summer are only available for a short time as they do not keep and indeed are best eaten ripe from the tree. Mid-season varieties, ready to be picked in early autumn will keep longer and in some cases up to December. The late season apples keep well for several months and consequently are available for a much longer period. A number of late season varieties, such as Golden Delicious, Granny Smith and Red Delicious, are now grown throughout the world – in both the northern and the southern hemispheres – and as a result are on sale all year round in our supermarkets and shops.

—THE—
APPLE
VARIETIES

Ashmead's Kernel
Long-esteemed English dessert variety. Quite russetted skin. Firm, white flesh, which mellows to an intense sweet-sharp, almost fruit drop flavour. Available: few UK farm shops; Dec-Feb.

Baldwin
Deep maroon flushed, large; multi-purpose. Keeps its shape when cooked and is recommended for pies; can be eaten fresh and was used for making cider. Available: USA; Dec-Apr.

Ben Davis
Dark red, large; dual purpose with sweet, firm flesh. Available: USA; Dec-Mar/May.

Blenheim Orange
Netted with russet and orange-red flush and stripes, it was favoured by Victorians for making 'Apple Charlotte', while smaller specimens were allowed to mellow and develop a characteristic crumbly texture and nutty flavour. Fresh fruit goes well with cheese. Cooked, it forms a stiff purée or retains its shape. Grown under the name Bénédictin in Normandy, France where it is valued for making 'Tarte aux Pommes'

and 'tarte Tatin'. Available: few UK farm shops, Germany, France; late Sept-Dec.

Braeburn
Red flushed and striped over greenish yellow with crisp to firm flesh and refreshing, fruity, quite perfumed taste. Available: worldwide; almost all year.

Bramley's Seedling

Bramley's Seedling
The best known English culinary variety, large, green with a slight flush. Cooks to a juicy purée with plenty of strong acidity and flavour, which is ideally suited to English pies, apple sauce, dumplings and baked apple. Available: UK; Sept-Jun.

Charles Ross
Handsomely flushed and striped in orange and red. Dual

purpose, cooked slices will retain their shape with a sweet, quite delicate flavour. Later in its season it makes a sweet, aromatic eater. Available: few UK farm shops; Sept-Dec.

Cox's Orange Pippin
England's most celebrated dessert variety. Flushed and striped in orange and red with a rich, intense, complex, aromatic flavour; sweet yet with plenty of balancing acidity and a deep cream-coloured, juicy flesh. Can be cooked – slices will retain shape, with a delicate flavour. Available: UK, northern Europe; Oct-Apr, New Zealand imports; May-July.

Cox's Orange Pippin

Crispin syn. Mutsu
Large, greenish yellow turning gold with crisp, deep creamy

6

flesh. Honeyed flavour at its best, very like Golden Delicious, but larger and with a coarser texture. When cooked, slices retain shape, with a sweet, very light taste. Available: USA, UK farm shops, Europe; Dec-Mar.

Delicious
Dark red with prominently crowned shape and the most widely grown of all varieties. Sweet, juicy, cream tinged green flesh, but often rather insipid; tough skin. Red Delicious, Starking, Red Chief are more highly coloured forms. Available: worldwide; all year.

Discovery
Bright red flush. Crisp, juicy flesh with a hint of strawberry flavour in well-ripened fruit. Available: UK; Aug-early Sept.

Discovery

Early Victoria
syn. Emneth Early
Pale greenish yellow. Cooking to a brisk, fruity, juicy fluff. Well suited to summer puddings such as 'Apple Snow'; when baked will puff up like a soufflé. Available: few UK farm shops; Aug-Sept.

Early Victoria

Egremont Russet
'Russet' of the UK high street, with a distinctive taste – nutty, yet almost smoky and sweet, quite firm flesh. Available: UK; Oct-Dec/Jan.

Ellison's Orange
Flushed and striped in orange and red. Juicy, brisk, quite soft flesh with a distinct aniseed flavour in well-ripened fruit. Available: UK farm shops; late Sept-Oct.

Empire
Red flush and waxy bloom. Crisp, juicy, sweet with quite scented flavour. Available: USA, Canada, imported into UK; Nov-Feb.

Fiesta
Attractive, orange red flush and stripes. Sweet, crisp flesh and plenty of rich flavour recalling its Cox's Orange Pippin parent. Available: UK; Oct-Mar.

Fortune syn. Laxton's Fortune
Red flushed and striped. Juicy, sweet, quite rich and lightly aromatic at its best. Available: UK farm shops; Sept-Oct.

Fuji
Pretty orange red flush. Crisp, firm, quite juicy flesh with honeyed sweetness. Available: worldwide; almost all year.

Gala
Bright pinky red flush and stripes over gold. Crisp, sweet flesh with a rich, honeyed, perfumed quality. Red Gala and Tenroy are more highly coloured forms. Available: worldwide; almost all year.

Golden Delicious
At best, sweet and honeyed with crisp, very juicy nearly yellow

flesh, but low in balancing acidity and can often taste flat and cloying. Dual purpose in many countries; when cooked keeps its shape well, with a light, sweet taste. Available: worldwide; all year.

Granny Smith
Bright green with brisk, crisp flesh, but often hard and acidic. Can be dual purpose; when cooked retains shape, but has mild flavour. Available: worldwide; all year.

Granny Smith

Gravenstein
Red flush over pale yellow, having a large, angular shape. Very juicy flesh and refreshing savoury taste. Can be dual purpose; slices retain shape when cooked and have a sweet, delicate taste; also used for juice. Available USA, northern Europe; Sept-Oct.

Gravenstein

Grimes Golden
Sweet, juicy, crisp yellow flesh that recalls its offspring Golden Delicious, but has a better, more complex flavour. Can be cooked; slices keep their shape. Available: USA; Nov-Feb.

Howgate Wonder
Large, red flushed and striped. Keeps its shape when cooked with a light taste but insipid in comparison to Bramley. Later in season, eaten fresh has a juicy, sweet and pleasant flavour. Available: UK farm shops; Nov-Mar.

Idared
Bright red flushed with sprightly taste, but can be flavourless and chewy. Dual purpose in USA and Europe; when cooked, slices will retain shape. Available: USA, Europe, small extent UK; Nov-Jun.

James Grieve
Red flush and stripes over pale yellow. Savoury, juicy, crisp yet melting flesh with strong acidity. Makes good juice and cooks well – as slices keep their shape with a sweet, delicate taste. Available: UK farm shops, northern Europe; Sept-Dec.

Jerseymac
Dark red flush and bloom of its McIntosh ancestor, but ripening earlier. Perfumed, sweet vinous flavour and sweet, melting, snow white flesh; tough skin. Available: USA, Europe; Sept-Nov.

Jonagold
Orange red flush and red stripes over gold; often quite large. Rich, honeyed, flavour, sweet and well balanced by acidity with crisp, juicy flesh. Well

suited to fresh fruit and vegetable salads. Jonagored is a more highly coloured form. Available: USA, Europe; Nov-April.

Jonagold

Jonathan

Bright crimson flush; crisp, sweet with plenty of refreshing acidity. Valued also for cooking in sauces and pies; slices will retain shape. Available: USA, small extent UK, Europe; Nov-Mar.

Kidd's Orange Red

Deep pinky crimson flush and stripes. Rich blend of sugar and acidity with intense aromatic flavour which mellows to a flowery rose petal quality, but in a poor year can be less interesting. Available: few UK farm shops; Nov-Jan.

Laxton's Superb

Deep red to purple flush over greenish yellow. Sweet, juicy finely textured flesh and some aromatic quality recalling its Cox parent. Available: UK farm shops; Nov-Jan.

Lobo

Deep maroon flushed McIntosh type with sweet, juicy, melting flesh. Available: USA, Canada, northern Europe, few UK farm shops; Sept-Nov.

Lodi

Pale greenish yellow, cooking to a sweet, very juicy, froth. Available: USA; late July-Aug.

Lodi

Lord Derby

Large, greenish yellow, angular shaped cooker. Strong, quite sharp taste when cooked and keeping a little of its form; good for pies. Available: UK farm shops; Sept-Dec.

Lord Lambourne

Bright red flush and stripes over greenish yellow. Crisp, juicy flesh with plenty of fruity flavour. Available: UK; Sept-Nov.

Macoun

Purplish red flush with heavy bloom like its McIntosh parent. Juicy, very sweet, pure white flesh perfumed sfrom anything between a strawberry, through to a vinous flavour. Available: USA, Canada; Oct-Dec/Feb.

Malling Kent

Dark orange red flush and stripes over greenish yellow. Quite rich and aromatic, but often less interesting. Can be dual purpose; slices will retain shape when cooked with sweet, light taste. Available: UK farm shops; Nov-Feb/Jun.

McIntosh

Canada's most famous variety with deep purplish red flush and a pronounced bloom. Melting, juicy, white flesh with a sweet, strawberry flavour turning vinous later. Available: USA, Canada, northern Europe, imported into UK; Oct-Jan and later.

Melrose
Shiny red with brisk refreshing taste and crisp, juicy flesh. Can be used early in the season for cooking and slices will retain their shape. Available: USA, France, imported into UK, few UK farm shops; Nov-Mar.

Melrose

Newton Wonder
Large, orange red flush over greenish yellow. Cooks to a

sharp juicy purée, but not as acidic as a Bramley. Suitable for all types of English puddings – pies, dumplings, baked apple and sauces. Mellows in a garden store to become a brisk eating apple; also good for mixed vegetable salads. Available: UK farm shops; Nov-Mar.

Newtown Pippin
Greenish yellow with crisp flesh and brisk taste which mellows in a home store to a distinct pineapple flavour. Valued also for cooking, keeping its shape, with a sweet good taste. Available: USA; Dec-Mar.

Northern Spy
Large, flushed dark red with a brisk, intense fruity flavour and crisp flesh. Dual purpose; slices keep shape when cooked. Available: USA, Canada; Nov-Mar.

Reine des Reinettes
Flushed and striped in orange and red over gold. Multipurpose – used for cooking and favoured for 'Tarte aux Pommes', also for making cider in Normandy. Known as King of the Pippins in UK, Gold Parmäne in Germany. Available: France, occasionally imported into UK; Sept-Dec.

Rhode Island Greening
Large, greenish yellow. When cooked, keeps shape with a sweet, good flavour; favoured for pies and sauces. Mellows to become a juicy, sprightly eater. Available: USA; Dec-Apr.

Rhode Island Greening

Ribston Pippin
The most popular Victorian dessert apple and probable parent of the well known Cox. Orange flush and red stripes over gold, patched with russet. Rich, intensely aromatic flavour, like a more robust Cox, with deep cream flesh. Available: few UK farm shops; Oct-Dec.

Rome Beauty
Deep red flush and stripes. Dual purpose. Keeps shape when cooked, sweet but mildly flavoured. Available: USA; Dec-Apr.

Saint Edmund's Pippin
syn. St Edmund's Russet
Light golden russet. Sweet, juicy, very rich densely textured, pale cream flesh. Available: UK farm shops; Sept-Oct.

Saint Edmund's Pippin

Spartan
Deep maroon flush with bloom. At best, perfumed, sweet flavour like a cross between a melon and a strawberry, but often rather bland; crisp juicy white flesh. Skin rather tough but makes an attractive contrast in fruit salads. Available: Canada, USA, UK; Nov-Mar.

Stayman's Winesap
Deep red skin like Winesap with juicy pale yellow flesh and a sprightly quality. Can be dual purpose. Available: USA, Europe; Jan-Mar.

Sturmer Pippin
Orange brown flush over greenish yellow. Crisp, juicy flesh, quite sweet, yet plenty of acidity and strong characteristic taste. Can be cooked and slices keep shape. Available: few Essex farm shops; Jan-March, imported from New Zealand to UK and Europe; May-Aug.

Tydeman's Early Worcester
syn. Tydeman's Early
Bright crimson with darker stripes. Very juicy, white flesh with some strawberry flavour when really ripe. Available: Canada, USA, southern Europe, few UK farm shops; Aug-Sept.

Wealthy
Bright red flush and stripes with sweet, soft, juicy flesh. Available: USA, Canada; Sept-Dec.

White Transparent
or Yellow Transparent
Pale yellow in colour, ripening by mid-July. Cooks to a sweet purée and also makes a refreshing, soft-fleshed eater with plenty of acidity. Available: USA, northern Europe; July-Aug.

Winesap
Dark red flush; sweet, juicy and fruity. Dual purpose in US. Available: USA, small extent Europe; Dec-Mar.

Worcester Pearmain
Perfectly ripe, bright red flushed. Sweet, strawberry flavour and firm, juicy white flesh, often chewy with little flavour. Available: UK; Sept-Oct.

Worcester Pearmain

CIDER APPLE SOUP

Serves 4-6

**500 g (*1 lb*) dessert apples, peeled,
cored and thinly sliced**
450 ml (¾ *pint*) vegetable or chicken stock
½ teaspoon ground cinnamon
¾ teaspoon ground ginger
2 tablespoons fresh white breadcrumbs
finely grated rind and juice of 1 lemon
150 ml (¼ *pint*) cider
150 ml (¼ *pint*) milk

TO GARNISH:

soured cream
a little ground cinnamon

Place apples in a saucepan with the vegetable or chicken stock, cinnamon, ginger, bread-crumbs, lemon rind and juice. Bring to the boil, then simmer gently for 10 minutes or until the apples are soft. Reserve some slices for garnish.

Purée the soup in a liquidizer or food processor, or rub through a sieve. Stir in the cider and milk.

Chill until needed. Serve in individual dishes, garnished with the reserved apple slices, soured cream and a little ground cinnamon.

CHESTNUT & APPLE SOUP

Serves 4

500 g (*1 lb*) chestnuts, skins slashed
1 tablespoon sunflower oil
1 onion, finely chopped
750 ml (*1¼ pints*) chicken stock
300 ml (*½ pint*) dry cider
**250 g (*8 oz*) cooking apples, peeled,
cored and sliced**
salt and freshly ground black pepper
flat leaf parsley, to garnish

Put the chestnuts in a large saucepan and cover with cold water. Bring to the boil and cook for 10 minutes. Drain and peel the chestnuts. Place in a clean pan, cover with water and cook for 20 minutes.

Put the oil in another large pan, add the onion and cook until soft, then add the stock, cider and apples.

Stir to mix the ingredients. Add the chestnuts with any of their cooking liquid left in the pan. Bring to the boil, reduce the heat, cover and simmer for about 15 minutes, until chestnuts are completely cooked. Blend in a liquidizer or food processor until smooth, or rub through a sieve. Season to taste and serve hot, garnished with flat leaf parsley.

Illustrated opposite

CURRIED APPLE SOUP

Serves 4

**500 g (*1 lb*) tart dessert apples, peeled,
cored and chopped
1 onion, sliced
2 sticks celery, thinly sliced
40 g (*1½ oz*) butter or margarine
2 teaspoons curry powder (mild or hot, to taste)
1 tablespoon chopped fresh mint
4 tablespoons lemon juice
600 ml (*1 pint*) chicken stock
300 ml (*½ pint*) milk or natural yogurt
salt and freshly ground black pepper
4 teaspoons sunflower seeds, to garnish**

In a large saucepan, gently fry apples, onion and celery in the fat, stirring occasionally, for 5 minutes. Increase the heat to moderate, stir in the curry powder, cook for 3 minutes. Add the mint and lemon juice and stir in the stock. Bring slowly to the boil, cover and simmer for 15 minutes, or until the apples are tender.

Purée the soup in a liquidizer or food processor, or rub through a sieve. Return soup to the rinsed pan and gradually pour in the milk or yogurt and bring slowly to simmering point. Do not allow to boil. Season to taste.

Serve the soup hot or cold, garnished with the sunflower seeds.

APPLE & CORIANDER SOUP

Serves 6

**25 g (*1 oz*) butter
1 onion, sliced
1 garlic clove, chopped
2 teaspoons ground coriander
1 potato, peeled and roughly chopped
750 g (*1½ lb*) tart dessert apples, peeled,
cored and chopped
900 ml (*1½ pints*) chicken stock
300 ml (*½ pint*) buttermilk
1 tablespoon lemon juice
2 tablespoons chopped fresh coriander or mint
50 g (*2 oz*) full-fat soft cheese
salt and freshly ground black pepper
fresh coriander or mint sprigs, to garnish**

Melt the butter in a saucepan, fry the onion and garlic over a moderate heat for 2 minutes. Stir in the coriander and cook for 1 minute longer, stirring. Add the potato and apples, stir well and cook for 2-3 minutes. Pour on the stock, stirring all the time, and then the buttermilk. Season to taste.

Bring to the boil, cover; simmer for 15 minutes. Stir in the lemon juice and coriander or mint. Purée the soup in a liquidizer or food processor, or rub through a sieve. Reheat the soup gently, adjust the seasoning if necessary. Serve topped with spoonfuls of soft cheese, garnished with sprigs of coriander or mint.

TURKEY KEBABS WITH APPLE

Serves 6

KEBABS:

**6 turkey escalopes,
total weight about 750 g (*1½ lb*)
6 rashers rindless streaky bacon,
halved lengthways
2 small green dessert apples, each cut
into 6 wedges
1 red, orange or yellow pepper, cored, seeded
and cut into 2.5 cm (*1 inch*) squares
1 green pepper, cored, seeded and cut into
2.5 cm (*1 inch*) squares
12 large cherry tomatoes, or 6 tomatoes, halved
thyme sprigs, to garnish**

MARINADE:

**2 teaspoons paprika
5 tablespoons olive oil
2 teaspoons dried thyme
salt and freshly ground black pepper**

Cut each turkey escalope crossways into four wide strips and place in a large shallow dish. To make the marinade, mix together the paprika, olive oil, dried thyme, and salt and pepper. Add to the turkey, making sure to thoroughly coat the turkey pieces. Cover the dish and leave to marinate for 1 hour.

After marinating, fold the strips of turkey two or three times to form squares, each about 2.5 cm (*1 inch*). Wrap a piece of bacon around half of these turkey squares.

Oil six long skewers and thread an apple wedge on to each. Continue to assemble the kebabs, alternating between the squares of bacon-wrapped turkey, plain turkey, peppers and the tomatoes, ending each kebab with an apple wedge.

Grill the kebabs over a hot barbecue, or under a preheated hot grill for 12-15 minutes, or until the turkey juices run clear, turning them over several times during cooking and brushing them with the remaining marinade.

Serve the kebabs with a rice salad, and garnish with sprigs of thyme.

ROAST PHEASANT FLAMBEED WITH CALVADOS

Serves 4

2 pheasants, preferably hen birds,
plucked and cleaned ready for the oven
1 large onion, quartered
50 g (*2 oz*) butter
4 tart dessert apples, peeled,
cored and thickly sliced
25 g (*1 oz*) plain flour
300 ml (*½ pint*) dry white wine
4 tablespoons Calvados
75 ml (*3 fl oz*) double cream
2 tablespoons chopped fresh parsley
salt and freshly ground black pepper

Place the prepared pheasants in a roasting tin. Tuck the onion quarters under the birds and sprinkle with a little salt and pepper. Dot with the butter and place in a preheated oven, 190°C (*375°F*), Gas Mark 5. Roast for about 45 minutes, or until the birds are cooked through and tender.

Add the apples to the tin 15-20 minutes before the end of the cooking time.

Have ready a warmed serving dish. Remove the pheasants from the roasting tin and transfer them to the dish. Place the apple slices in a separate dish and keep them hot while making the Calvados sauce.

Stir the flour into the pan juices and cook over a moderate heat for 1 minute. Stir in the dry white wine and bring to the boil, stirring all the time. Remove from the heat.

Heat the Calvados in a small saucepan until it is just warm, set it alight and then, when the flames die down, add it to the sauce. Stir in the double cream and chopped parsley and adjust the seasoning to taste, then reheat the sauce gently without boiling.

Pour a little of the sauce around the pheasants and arrange the apples in the dish. Serve the pheasants accompanied by game chips and fresh green vegetables, with the remaining sauce served separately.

Illustrated opposite

BAKED CHICKEN WITH APPLES

Serves 4

50 g (*2 oz*) raisins
50 g (*2 oz*) butter
4 chicken portions
500 g (*1 lb*) dessert apples, such as Granny Smiths, peeled, cored and sliced
2 tablespoons lemon juice
6 tablespoons dry vermouth
1 teaspoon cinnamon
125 ml (*4 fl oz*) double cream
salt and freshly ground black pepper

Soak the raisins for 1 hour in warm water. Heat half the butter in a frying pan and brown the chicken portions on all sides. Remove to a plate and season well.

Add the remaining butter and apple slices to the frying pan and brown lightly. Place half the apples in the bottom of a casserole and arrange the chicken on top.

Mix the lemon juice, vermouth, salt and pepper, cinnamon and drained raisins. Place the remaining apples around the chicken, season and pour the raisin mixture over the chicken and apples. Cover and bake in a preheated oven, 160°C (*325°F*), Gas Mark 3, for about 1 hour. Stir in the cream and return to the oven to heat through for 5 minutes. Adjust the seasoning to taste and serve.

TROUT WITH APPLES

Serves 4

4 large rainbow trout, cleaned
1 tablespoon lemon juice
4 rosemary sprigs
75 g (*3 oz*) butter
2 dessert apples, cored and thickly sliced
freshly ground black pepper

TO GARNISH:

1 lemon, quartered
chopped fresh parsley

Sprinkle the inside of each trout with plenty of pepper and the lemon juice and place a sprig of rosemary in the cavity.

Melt 50 g (*2 oz*) of the butter in a large frying pan, add the trout and fry over a moderate heat for 12-15 minutes until tender. Using a wooden spatula or fish slice, turn the fish over once during cooking, taking care not to break the skin. Transfer to a warm serving dish. Add the remaining butter to the pan and fry the apples. Cook for a further 4-5 minutes, turning the apples once, until golden.

Serve the fish surrounded by the apples and garnished with the lemon wedges dipped along the edges, in the parsley.

PORK CHOPS NORMANDY-STYLE

Serves 4

4 loin pork chops, trimmed of fat
1 tablespoon sunflower oil
25 g (*1 oz*) butter
2 onions, sliced
1 garlic clove, crushed
2 small cooking apples, peeled, cored and sliced
1 tablespoon plain flour
250 ml (*8 fl oz*) sweet cider
1 tablespoon clear honey
1 tablespoon brandy (optional)
1 teaspoon fresh chopped thyme
4 tablespoons double cream
salt and freshly ground black pepper

Fry chops in the oil in a frying pan over a moderately high heat for 3 minutes each side. Transfer to a casserole. Add half the butter to the pan, fry onions and garlic over a moderate heat for 3 minutes. Transfer to the casserole. Fry apple slices in pan 1 minute each side and add to the casserole.

Melt the remaining butter, stir in the flour, cook for a few seconds. Stir in the cider, honey and brandy, if using. Bring to the boil, stirring continously. Season to taste. Add to the casserole with the thyme. Cover and cook in a preheated oven, 190°C (*375°F*), Gas Mark 5, for 35 minutes. Skim off the surface fat, stir in the cream. Adjust seasoning to taste, serve.

PORK & APPLE PASTIES

Serves 4

250 g (*8 oz*) lean pork, finely cubed
1 small cooking apple, peeled, cored and grated
1 onion, chopped
½ teaspoon dried sage
2 tablespoons dry cider or chicken stock
salt and freshly ground black pepper
milk, to glaze
PASTRY:
250 g (*8 oz*) plain flour
pinch of salt
125 g (*4 oz*) margarine
2-3 tablespoons cold water

For the pastry, place flour and salt in a bowl. Lightly rub in margarine until mixture resembles fine breadcrumbs. Sprinkle 2 tablespoons water over, mix to form a dough, adding extra water, if necessary. Knead lightly and chill.

Mix together the remaining ingredients and season to taste. Divide pastry into four, roll each piece out to a 15 cm (*6 inch*) circle. Divide filling between circles, dampen edges with water and bring together over the filling. Seal, pleat edges and place on greased baking tray. Brush with milk, bake in preheated oven, 200°C (*400°F*), Gas Mark 6, for 20 minutes. Reduce heat to 180°C (*350°F*), Gas Mark 4, bake for further 20-30 minutes. Serve hot.

APPLE, DATE & CELERY SALAD

Serves 4

1 head celery, sliced into 1 cm (½ *inch*) pieces
125 g (*4 oz*) stoned dates, thinly sliced
250 g (*8 oz*) tart apples, cored and cut
into 1 cm (½ *inch*) cubes
25 g (*1 oz*) pistachio nuts, chopped

DRESSING:

2 tablespoons clear honey
300 ml (½ *pint*) natural yogurt
1 tablespoon finely chopped fresh mint

Place the sliced celery, dates and apple cubes in a salad bowl.

For the dressing, combine the honey, yogurt and mint in a small bowl. Pour over the celery and fruit and toss gently.

Serve the salad chilled, sprinkled with chopped pistachio nuts.

ORCHARD SALAD

Serves 4-6

grated rind and juice of 2 small oranges
1 tablespoon chopped fresh mint or parsley
375 g (*12 oz*) firm pears, quartered,
cored and sliced
375 g (*12 oz*) dessert apples, such as Cox's
or Worcesters, quartered, cored and sliced
125 g (*4 oz*) blackberries
50 g (*2 oz*) redcurrants
50 g (*2 oz*) roasted hazelnuts,
roughly chopped
salt and freshly ground black pepper
salad leaves, to serve

Place the orange rind and orange juice in a mixing bowl. Stir in the mint or parsley and season to taste. Add the sliced pears and apples and toss well.

Add the blackberries, redcurrants and hazelnuts, toss all together and serve on a bed of salad leaves.

Serve the salad as an accompaniment to rich meats such as pork or duck.

Illustrated opposite

KIPPER & APPLE SALAD

Serves 4

425 g (*14 oz*) kipper fillets
3 tablespoons lemon juice
2 teaspoons sunflower oil
1 teaspoon ground coriander (optional)
50 g (*2 oz*) long-grain brown rice, washed
450 ml (*¾ pint*) water
2 tablespoons chopped fresh parsley
175 g (*6 oz*) red dessert apple, cored and diced
pinch of freshly ground black pepper

TO SERVE:

1 head of Chinese leaves, about 500 g (*1 lb*)
1 lemon, cut into wedges (optional)

Poach the kipper fillets for 5 minutes in simmering water to cover. Drain, scrape off the skin and cut into bite-sized pieces. Place the fish in a serving dish and pour over the lemon juice, oil and coriander, if using. Chill for 3-4 hours, stirring occasionally.

Bring the rice and water to the boil in a saucepan. Cover and simmer 35-45 minutes, until the rice is tender. Drain well. Rinse in hot water and drain again. Combine the rice while still warm with the parsley and pepper.

To serve, shred the Chinese leaves and divide between four plates. Top with spoonfuls of rice and arrange pieces of apple and kipper on top. Garnish with lemon wedges, if liked.

CHICKEN & APPLE CURRY MAYONNAISE

Serves 4-6

500 g (*1 lb*) boneless, skinless cooked chicken
or turkey, cut into cubes
2 red dessert apples, cut into small cubes
25 g (*1 oz*) sultanas or raisins
25 g (*1 oz*) roasted, salted peanuts
6 tablespoons mayonnaise
1 teaspoon medium or mild curry powder
½ teaspoon mild chilli powder
1 tablespoon lime or lemon juice
salt and freshly ground black pepper
crisp lettuce leaves, to serve
coriander leaves, to garnish

Place all the ingredients, except the salt, pepper, lettuce leaves and coriander, in a large mixing bowl and mix thoroughly. Season to taste with salt and pepper.

Line a serving dish or individual serving dishes with the lettuce leaves and spoon in the curried chicken mixture. Garnish with coriander leaves.

APPLE & AVOCADO PASTA SALAD

Serves 4-6

250 g *(8 oz)* small pasta shapes, such as
bows, shells or twists
1 teaspoon sunflower oil
1 avocado
2 tablespoons lemon juice
3 sticks celery, sliced
2 red dessert apples, cored and thinly sliced
4 tablespoons French dressing
2 tablespoons snipped fresh chives

Cook the pasta shapes in lightly salted boiling water with the oil, according to the packet instructions, until *al dente*. Drain and cool under cold water. Drain again thoroughly.

Peel and stone the avocado, then slice thinly or chop into cubes. Toss in the lemon juice to prevent it turning brown.

Mix the pasta with the avocado, celery and apple in a serving bowl. Add the dressing and chives and toss gently to coat and mix. Garnish with any extra chives.

WALDORF SALAD

Serves 6

6 Granny Smith apples, peeled,
cored and cut into small cubes
3 tablespoons lemon juice, strained
250 g *(8 oz)* can pineapple slices in
natural juice, drained
75 g *(3 oz)* walnuts, coarsely chopped
6 sticks celery, sliced
125 ml *(4 fl oz)* mayonnaise
75 ml *(3 fl oz)* soured cream
2 teaspoons clear honey
salt

Place the apple cubes in a large bowl and toss with the lemon juice. Cut the pineapple into small pieces and add to the bowl with the walnuts and celery.

Combine the mayonnaise, soured cream and honey with salt to taste and fold through the apple mixture. Cover and chill for 1-2 hours to blend and mellow the flavours. Bring to room temperature to serve.

APPLE & CELERIAC SALAD

Serves 6

1 celeriac, about 750 g (*1½ lb*),
peeled and quartered
2 tablespoons lemon juice
1 teaspoon salt
5 tablespoons mayonnaise
1 tablespoon finely chopped fresh chervil
or borage
1 tablespoon finely chopped fresh parsley
2 crisp red dessert apples, cored
and thinly sliced into rings
125 g (*4 oz*) salted cashew nuts, finely chopped

Put the celeriac in a saucepan, add the lemon juice and salt and cover with water. Bring to the boil, reduce the heat and cook for about 30 minutes, until tender, but still firm. Drain thoroughly, allow to cool, then slice thinly.

Mix together the mayonnaise, chervil or borage and parsley. Add the apple and celeriac slices and stir to coat. Transfer to a salad bowl. Sprinkle the cashew nuts over the top and serve.

APPLE TREE SALAD

Serves 4-6

2 red dessert apples, cored and thinly sliced
2 teaspoons lemon juice
250 g (*8 oz*) button mushrooms, thinly sliced
250 g (*8 oz*) black grapes, halved and seeded
2 carrots, scraped and grated
2 sticks celery, sliced
2 tablespoons roasted sesame seeds

DRESSING:

2 tablespoons olive oil
1 tablespoon cloudy apple juice
2 tablespoons soured cream
salt and freshly ground black pepper

Mix all of the dressing ingredients together until well blended.

Toss the apples in the lemon juice. Mix together the apple and mushroom slices, the grapes, carrots and celery. Sprinkle with the sesame seeds.

Pour on the dressing and mix well to serve. Alternatively, serve the dressing separately.

Illustrated opposite

APPLE & SWEET POTATO CASSEROLE

Serves 4-6

2 sweet potatoes, about 900 g (*2 lb*)
4 small apples, cored and sliced into rings
2-3 tablespoons caster sugar
2 tablespoons coarsely chopped pecan
or cashew nuts
50 g (*2 oz*) butter
1 teaspoon salt
pinch of grated nutmeg

Place the whole sweet potatoes in a large saucepan, cover with boiling water, bring back to the boil, lower the heat and cook for about 25-30 minutes or until barely tender. Rinse under cold water, peel and cut lengthways into thick slices.

Fill a greased ovenproof dish with alternate layers of sweet potato and apple and sprinkle with the sugar and nuts.

Melt the butter in a small pan, season with the salt and nutmeg and pour over the sweet potato and apple mixture.

Cook in a preheated oven, 200°C (*400°F*), Gas Mark 6, for 20-25 minutes. Serve immediately as a tasty vegetable dish, perfect with crisp roasted pork.

APPLE & RED CABBAGE

Serves 8

1 head red cabbage, about 1.5 kg (*3 lb*),
finely shredded
50 g (*2 oz*) fat salt pork, diced, or butter
2 Spanish onions, thinly sliced
2 tablespoons brown sugar
250 g (*8 oz*) tart dessert apples, peeled,
cored and chopped
75 ml (*3 fl oz*) vegetable stock
125 ml (*4 fl oz*) red wine
3 tablespoons wine or cider vinegar
1 small raw beetroot, coarsely grated
salt and freshly ground black pepper

Cover cabbage with boiling water, set aside. In a large heavy-based saucepan, sauté pork until the fat runs, or melt the butter. Add the onions, fry, stirring frequently, until soft and transparent. Stir in the sugar and continue to fry gently until the onions are caramelized and golden. Take care not to let the sugar burn.

Drain the cabbage well. Add it to the pan with the apples, stock, wine and vinegar. Mix well. Season generously with salt and pepper. Cover tightly and cook gently for 1½ hours, stirring occasionally. Mix in the grated beetroot – this transforms the colour – and continue to cook, covered, for 30 minutes longer, or until the cabbage is soft. Adjust the seasoning if necessary, and serve very hot.

APPLE & STILTON STUFFED ONIONS

Serves 4

4 large onions, about 250 g (*8 oz*) each
175 g (*6 oz*) cooking apple, peeled,
cored and chopped
50 g (*2 oz*) fresh breadcrumbs
125 g (*4 oz*) blue Stilton, finely crumbled
1 bunch watercress
50 g (*2 oz*) butter
salt and freshly ground black pepper

Peel the onions, then cook in a saucepan of boiling water for 15 minutes, until just tender. Drain, allow to cool so they can be handled.

Mix the apples with breadcrumbs and cheese. Reserve four sprigs of watercress, trim and chop remainder and add to cheese mixture.

Remove the middle of each onion – this is easiest if you gradually scoop out the layers of onion with a teaspoon. Leave an unbroken shell about two layers thick. Chop the scooped-out onion and add to the cheese mixture. Mix well and season to taste, then press the mixture into the onion shells.

Stand onions in an ovenproof dish, dot with a little butter. Bake in a preheated oven, 180°C (*350°F*), Gas Mark 4, for 45 minutes, or until stuffing is cooked through. Serve garnished with reserved watercress sprigs.

FENNEL BRAISED WITH APPLE

Serves 4

2 large fennel bulbs, quartered lengthways
1 large cooking apple, peeled, cored and sliced
150 ml (*¼ pint*) chicken stock
1 tablespoon lemon juice
salt and freshly ground black pepper
1 tablespoon chopped parsley, to garnish

Place the fennel quarters in a casserole or ovenproof dish. Add the apple to the casserole with the chicken stock, lemon juice and salt and pepper.

Cover and bake in a preheated oven, 180°C (*350°F*), Gas Mark 4, for 30 minutes, or until the fennel is tender, but not soft.

Drain the stock into a small saucepan and boil for about 3 minutes, or until it is reduced to 3 tablespoons. Pour the sauce over the fennel, sprinkle with chopped parsley and serve – ideal with pork or fish.

FRENCH APPLE TART

Serves 4-6

PASTRY:

150 g (*5 oz*) plain flour
pinch of salt
65 g (*2½ oz*) butter, cut into small pieces
1 tablespoon caster sugar
2 teaspoons ground almonds
1 egg yolk
2-3 tablespoons cold water

FILLING:

500 g (*1 lb*) cooking apples, cooked
unsweetened and puréed
50 g (*2 oz*) sugar
grated rind of ½ a lemon
2 cooking apples, peeled, cored
and thinly sliced

GLAZE:

1 tablespoon lemon juice
2-3 tablespoons icing sugar

To make the pastry, sift the flour and salt into a bowl, add the butter and using the fingertips, rub the fat and flour together until it resembles fine breadcrumbs; add the sugar and almonds. Stir in the egg yolk and enough cold water to mix to a stiff dough with a palette knife. Turn out on to a floured surface and knead lightly for 1 minute. Wrap in foil and chill in the refrigerator for 30 minutes.

Roll out the pastry on a floured surface and use to line a 20 cm (*8 inch*) flan ring, set on a baking tray.

Add the sugar and lemon rind to the apple purée and spoon into the flan case. Arrange the sliced apples neatly over the surface. Brush them with lemon juice and sprinkle with the icing sugar.

Bake the tart in a preheated oven, 220°C (*425°F*), Gas Mark 7, for 25-30 minutes or until the pastry is cooked through and the apples are coloured.

Serve warm or cold with whipped cream.

Illustrated opposite

FARMHOUSE FRUIT PIE

Serves 6

PASTRY:

175 g (*6 oz*) plain flour
pinch of salt
75 g (*3 oz*) butter or margarine, cut
into small pieces
1½-2 tablespoons water

FILLING:

2 cooking apples, peeled, cored and thinly sliced
2 pears, peeled, cored and thinly sliced
2 tablespoons golden syrup, melted
1 tablespoon redcurrant jelly, melted
¼ teaspoon ground mixed spice
25-50 g (*1-2 oz*) sultanas
25 g (*1 oz*) demerara sugar

TOPPING:

200 g (*7 oz*) packet frozen puff pastry, thawed
beaten egg, to glaze

To make the pastry, sift the flour and salt into a large bowl, add the butter or margarine and rub in until the mixture resembles fine breadcrumbs. Add enough water to form a firm dough. Knead lightly until it is smooth and free from cracks.

Roll out pastry on a lightly floured surface to a round large enough to line the base and sides of a 20 cm (*8 inch*) loose-based fluted flan tin, allowing the pastry to over-hang the edge of the tin slightly. Chill until needed.

To make the filling, mix the sliced apples and pears with the golden syrup, redcurrant jelly, mixed spice, sultanas and demerara sugar. Spoon into the pastry-lined tin.

For the topping, roll out the puff pastry to a round large enough to cover the pie. Dampen the edge of the pastry in the tin and place the puff pastry lid in position. Seal the edges together well then trim neatly. Knock up and flute the edges.

Glaze the pastry with beaten egg then lightly cut into it to give a lattice pattern, using a sharp pointed knife. Reroll the puff pastry trimmings and cut into leaf shapes for decoration. Position the leaves on the pie and brush with beaten egg.

Cook on a preheated baking sheet in a preheated oven, 200°C (*400°F*), Gas Mark 6, for 35-40 minutes until the pastry is risen and golden brown. Cover with foil and reduce the heat to 180°C (*350°F*), Gas Mark 4, and continue cooking for a further 15 minutes.

Cool slightly in the tin on a wire tray, then remove the sides of the tin, leaving the pie on the tin base. Serve hot or cold with custard, cream or ice-cream.

APPLE MERINGUE PIE

Serves 4-6

**500 g (*1 lb*) cooking apples, peeled,
cored and sliced
150 g (*5 oz*) caster sugar
25 g (*1 oz*) butter
grated rind of 1 lemon
150 ml (*¼ pint*) water
2 eggs, separated**

PASTRY:

**175 g (*6 oz*) plain flour
pinch of salt
75 g (*3 oz*) butter or margarine
1½-2 tablespoons water**

To make the pastry, sift the flour and salt into a bowl. Add the fat, cut into small pieces, and rub in until the mixture resembles fine breadcrumbs. Add enough water to form a firm dough. Knead lightly until smooth and free from cracks.

Roll out the pastry on a lightly floured work surface to a round large enough to line the base and sides of a 20 cm (*8 inch*) loose-based fluted flan tin.

Bake blind as follows. Line the pastry case with greaseproof paper and cover with a layer of dried beans to prevent the base blistering. Place in a preheated oven, 200°C (*400°F*), Gas Mark 6, for 10-15 minutes until the sides of

the flan are set and golden. Remove the lining paper and beans (which can be reused) and return the flan to the oven for about 5 minutes or until the base is crisp. Allow the pastry case to cool.

Put the apples in a saucepan with 50 g (*2 oz*) of the caster sugar, butter, lemon rind and water. Cook gently until the apples are tender, then beat to a smooth purée.

Cool the mixture slightly, then beat in the egg yolks. Put the mixture into the pastry case. Place in the oven and bake at 180°C (*350°F*), Gas Mark 4, for 20 minutes.

Whisk the egg whites until stiff, whisk in the remaining caster sugar, then spread the meringue over the top of the apples. Return to the oven for 15-20 minutes until golden. Serve hot or cold with pouring cream.

APPLE & BERRY CRUMB PIE

Serves 6-8

PASTRY:

175 g (*6 oz*) plain flour
pinch of salt
75 g (*3 oz*) butter or margarine,
cut into small pieces
1½-2 tablespoons water

FILLING:

275 g (*9 oz*) peeled and thickly sliced apples
200 g (*7 oz*) cranberries
125 g (*4 oz*) caster sugar
175 g (*6 oz*) plain flour
75 g (*3 oz*) butter
¾ teaspoon ground cinnamon
½ teaspoon grated lemon rind
75 g (*3 oz*) light brown sugar

LIQUEUR CREAM:

375 ml (*13 fl oz*) whipping cream
sifted icing sugar, to taste
Cointreau, Grand Marnier
or other liqueur, to taste

To make the pastry, sift the flour and salt into a bowl, add the fat and rub in until the mixture resembles fine breadcrumbs. Add enough water to form a firm dough. Knead lightly until smooth and free from cracks.

Roll out the pastry on a lightly floured surface to a round large enough to line the base and sides of a 20-23 cm (*8-9 inch*) loose-based fluted flan tin. Chill until required.

For the filling, toss the apples and cranberries with the caster sugar and put into the pie shell. Place the flour, butter, cinnamon and lemon rind in a bowl, then rub together until crumbly. Stir in the brown sugar. Sprinkle evenly over the fruit and pat down lightly.

Bake in a preheated oven, 180°C (*350°F*), Gas Mark 4, for 45 minutes or until the crumb topping and pastry are golden brown.

To make the liqueur cream, whip the cream until it begins to thicken. Sweeten to taste with sifted icing sugar and add a spoonful or two of Cointreau or other liqueur to taste, then continue whipping until thick. Serve the pie warm or cold, with the liqueur cream.

Illustrated opposite

APPLE & APRICOT PLAIT

Serves 6-8

250 g (*8 oz*) packet frozen puff pastry, thawed
300 g (*10 oz*) fresh apricots, halved,
stoned and quartered
1 large cooking apple, peeled, cored and diced
2 tablespoons caster sugar
50 g (*2 oz*) flaked almonds
1 egg, beaten
1 tablespoon demerara sugar
sifted icing sugar, to serve

Roll out the pastry to a rectangle 20 x 30 cm (*9 x 12 inches*) in size. Make diagonal slashes at 1.5 cm (*¾ inch*) intervals along both sides of the length of the rectangle, leaving a 10 cm (*4 inch*) panel down the centre.

Mix together the fruit, caster sugar and almonds, and spread down the centre panel. Turn the two ends of the pastry in, then plait the pastry strips over the filling, securing the last two strips under the plait with beaten egg.

Place on a baking sheet, brush with beaten egg and sprinkle with demerara. Bake in a preheated oven, 200°C (*400°F*), Gas Mark 6, for 20 minutes, until well risen, then reduce the heat to 180°C (*350°F*), Gas Mark 4, and continue cooking for 15-20 minutes, until golden. Dust with icing sugar and serve with whipped cream.

SPICED APPLE TURNOVERS

Serves 6

675 g (*1½ lb*) cooking apples, peeled,
cored and chopped
140 g (*4½ oz*) soft brown sugar
1 teaspoon ground cinnamon
1 tablespoon raisins
500 g (*1 lb*) packet frozen puff pastry, thawed
beaten egg yolk, to glaze

Cook the apples, sugar, cinnamon and raisins in a little water until the mixture forms a compôte. Allow to cool.

Roll out the puff pastry and cut out six 15 cm (*6 inch*) circles. Brush the edges with water. Spoon the cold apple into the middle of each circle. Fold and seal the edges of the pastry, enclosing the apple, and crimp the edges neatly. Brush the top of each turnover with lightly beaten egg yolk and decorate with the point of a sharp knife.

Lay the turnovers on a baking sheet sprinkled with water, and bake in a preheated oven, 220°C (*425°F*), Gas Mark 7, for 20 minutes. Serve hot or cold with cream.

CREAM & APPLE TART

Serves 6-8

PASTRY:

250 g (*8 oz*) plain flour
pinch of salt
125 g (*4 oz*) butter or margarine
2-3 tablespoons water

CUSTARD CREAM:

3 tablespoons sugar
pinch of salt
3 tablespoons cornflour
150 ml (*¼ pint*) milk
150 ml (*¼ pint*) single cream
3 egg yolks, lightly beaten
1 tablespoon brandy, apricot or orange
liqueur, or 1 teaspoon vanilla essence
150 ml (*¼ pint*) double or whipping cream

APPLES:

1 tablespoon brandy
1 teaspoon lemon juice
2 tablespoons cold water
4 large, fragrant dessert apples, peeled,
cored and very thinly sliced
2 tablespoons melted butter
2 tablespoons caster sugar, sifted

Make the pastry case and bake blind as described on page 31, using a 25 cm (*10 inch*) loose-based fluted flan tin.

For the custard cream, mix the sugar, salt and cornflour together in a heavy-based saucepan and blend in the milk and single cream. Bring the mixture to the boil, stirring, and continue to simmer for 3-4 minutes. Remove the pan from the heat and cool the mixture slightly, stirring. Then gradually beat in the egg yolks.

Return the pan to a very low heat and cook, stirring constantly, for 3-4 minutes or until the custard is very thick and smooth. Do not let the custard bubble. Stir in the brandy, liqueur or vanilla essence. Cool, beating occasionally to prevent a skin forming on top. Set aside in a covered bowl until ready to use.

For the apples, mix the brandy, lemon juice and water in a large bowl. Coat the apples in the brandy mixture.

Whisk the double or whipping cream stiffly and fold it into the custard. Spread the custard cream over the base of the cooked pastry case. Arrange the apple slices in overlapping concentric circles over the top, shaking them free of excess moisture as you lift them out of the bowl. Brush the apples with melted butter and dust with caster sugar.

Place the tart under a moderate grill and grill steadily for 10 minutes, or until the surface is golden and lightly caramelized. Regulate the heat of the grill so that the sides of the pastry case do not get too brown before the top is caramelized, or shield the pastry with a little crumpled foil. Serve lukewarm, cold or chilled, on the day it is made.

APPLE STRUDEL

Serves 8-10

DOUGH:

250 g (*8 oz*) plain flour
½ teaspoon salt
1 egg, lightly beaten
2 tablespoons sunflower oil
3 tablespoons warm water

FILLING:

125 g (*4 oz*) butter
50 g (*2 oz*) fresh white breadcrumbs
750 g (*1½ lb*) cooking apples, peeled,
cored and coarsely grated
50 g (*2 oz*) raisins
50 g (*2 oz*) currants
75 g (*3 oz*) caster sugar
½ teaspoon ground cinnamon
2 teaspoons finely grated lemon rind
sifted icing sugar, to serve

Sieve together the flour and salt. Make a well in the centre and pour in the egg and oil. Add the water gradually, stirring with a fork, to make a soft sticky dough. Work the dough in the bowl until it leaves the sides clean, then turn out on to a lightly floured surface and knead for about 15 minutes or until the dough feels smooth and elastic. Form into a ball, place in a bowl and cover with a warm cloth. Leave to rest for 1 hour.

Melt half the butter in a saucepan and fry the breadcrumbs until they are crisp and golden. Add the apples, raisins, currants, caster sugar, cinnamon and lemon rind.

Warm a rolling pin, and flour a large clean tea towel. Place the dough on the towel and roll it out to a rectangle as thinly as possible, lifting and turning it to prevent it from sticking to the cloth. Using the backs of your hands, gently stretch the dough, working from the centre to the outside until it is paper thin – you should be able to read through the dough, but to do this takes years of practice and patience. Then leave the dough to rest for 15 minutes.

Melt the remaining butter and use most of it to brush all over the dough. Spread the filling on the dough to within 2.5 cm (*1 inch*) of the edges. Lift the two corners of the tea towel nearest to you and roll the dough away from you. Place the dough on a greased baking sheet and form into a horseshoe. Brush all over with the remaining melted butter. Bake in a preheated oven, 200°C (*400°F*), Gas Mark 6, for about 20 minutes, then reduce the heat to 180°C (*350°F*), Gas Mark 4, for a further 30 minutes.

Serve warm or cold, dusted with icing sugar and cut into thick slices.

Illustrated opposite

BAKED APPLES WITH DATES

Serves 4

4 large cooking apples, cored
50 g (*2 oz*) dates, stoned and chopped
25 g (*1 oz*) raisins
8 unblanched almonds, chopped
25 g (*1 oz*) soft brown sugar
½ teaspoon ground cinnamon
4 tablespoons cider

Make a shallow cut round the middle of each cooking apple.

Mix together the dates, raisins, almonds, sugar and cinnamon and use to fill the apple cavities, pressing down firmly.

Place in an ovenproof dish and add the cider. Bake in a preheated oven, 180°C (*350°F*), Gas Mark 4, for 50-60 minutes, until soft. Serve hot with cream or custard.

Illustrated on page 1

APPLE & LEMON SPONGE PUDDING

Serves 6

375 g (*12 oz*) peeled and thinly
sliced cooking apples
150 g (*5 oz*) caster sugar
75 g (*3 oz*) soft margarine
50 g (*2 oz*) self-raising flour
2 eggs, separated
grated rind and juice of 1 large lemon
200 ml (*7 fl oz*) milk

Place the apples in a 1.5 litre *(2½ pint)* ovenproof dish. Sprinkle with 25 g *(1 oz)* of the sugar.

Cream the remaining sugar with the margarine. Stir in the flour, egg yolks, lemon rind and juice and mix well. Gradually blend in the milk. Whisk the egg whites until stiff but not dry. Fold into the lemon mixture and then pour over the apples.

Bake in a preheated oven, 160°C (*325°F*), Gas Mark 3, for 45 minutes, until golden brown – the pudding separates to give a fluffy sponge topping over an apple base. Serve warm with pouring cream.

CREPES AUX POMMES

Makes 8

75 g (*3 oz*) butter
4 small dessert apples, peeled,
cored and sliced
2 tablespoons icing sugar

BATTER:

65 g (*2½ oz*) plain flour
2 eggs, lightly beaten
150 ml (*¼ pint*) milk
1½ tablespoons melted butter

To make the batter, sift the flour into a bowl. Beat in the eggs one at a time. Beat in the milk until you obtain a smooth batter, then whisk in the butter. Leave to stand for 2 hours, before using.

For each apple pancake, melt a knob of butter in a 20 cm (*8 inch*) frying pan. Arrange half a sliced apple in the pan. Fry on one side until soft and golden, then turn over and fry on the other side.

Pour enough pancake batter into the pan to cover the bottom. Cook one side and turn carefully. While the second side is cooking, sprinkle a little icing sugar over the pancake. Slip it on to a dessert plate and glaze under a hot grill for a few seconds. Repeat with the rest of the apples and pancake batter. Serve the pancakes warm with cream or ice-cream.

APPLE NUT CRUMBLE

Serves 4

3-4 large dessert apples, about 875 g (*1¼ lb*)
peeled, cored and roughly chopped
65 g (*2½ oz*) light brown sugar
75 g (*3 oz*) plain wholemeal flour
75 g (*3 oz*) plain flour
½ teaspoon ground cardamom (optional)
½ teaspoon mixed spice
1 teaspoon ground cinnamon
¼ teaspoon grated nutmeg
75 g (*3 oz*) butter, softened
50 g (*2 oz*) shelled Brazil nuts, chopped

Place the apples in a large bowl, sprinkle with 1 tablespoon of the sugar and set aside.

Mix the flours and spices together in a large mixing bowl and rub in the butter until the mixture resembles fine breadcrumbs. Stir in the remaining sugar.

Line the bottom of a buttered ovenproof dish with one-third of the crumble mixture. Put the apples and any juice on top. Sprinkle with the remaining crumble mixture. Scatter over the chopped Brazil nuts.

Cover with foil and bake in a preheated oven, 200°C (*400°F*), Gas Mark 6, for 35 minutes, removing the foil for the last 10 minutes. Serve hot with custard.

TARTE TATIN

Serves 6

PASTRY:

175 g (*6 oz*) plain flour, sifted

75 g (*3 oz*) butter

25 g (*1 oz*) sugar

1 egg yolk

FILLING:

50 g (*2 oz*) butter

50 g (*2 oz*) sugar

1 kg (*2 lb*) dessert apples, peeled,

cored and quartered

1 teaspoon grated nutmeg, for sprinkling

To make the pastry, place the flour in a bowl, rub in the butter until mixture resembles fine breadcrumbs. Stir in the sugar, then egg yolk to make a short, sweet pastry. Chill briefly.

For the filling, melt butter in an 18 cm (*7 inch*) *tarte tatin* pan or a deep sandwich tin. Stir the sugar into the butter, cook gently until it dissolves and begins to caramelize. Remove from heat, then pack apples tightly into pan.

Roll pastry into a circle slightly larger than the pan. Lift over the apples, tucking edges down into the pan. Bake in a preheated oven, 200°C (*400°F*), Gas Mark 6, for 30 minutes, or until pastry is cooked. Invert on to a plate, sprinkle with nutmeg and serve hot or warm.

Illustrated on front jacket

CRUNCHY CINNAMON PUDDING

Serves 4

250 g (*8 oz*) fresh breadcrumbs

2-3 teaspoons ground cinnamon

75 g (*3 oz*) brown sugar

75 g (*3 oz*) butter, melted

4 cooking apples, peeled, cored and quartered

125 ml (*4 fl oz*) water

3 tablespoons caster sugar

250 ml (*8 fl oz*) double cream

150 ml (*¼ pint*) natural yogurt

TO SERVE:

whipped cream

chocolate curls

Stir breadcrumbs, cinnamon and brown sugar into the butter in a frying pan and stir over a medium heat until crisp and toffee-like. Cool.

Poach apples in the water with 1 tablespoon of the caster sugar. When soft, purée in a liquidizer or food processor, or rub through a sieve, cool. Whip cream with remaining caster sugar until thick, then stir in the yogurt. In individual dishes or one large glass bowl, make layers of apple, crumbs and cream, ending with a layer of crumbs. Chill, serve decorated with whipped cream and chocolate.

Illustrated opposite

OZARK PUDDING

Serves 4

1 egg
125 g (*4 oz*) sugar
1 tablespoon plain flour
1½ teaspoons baking powder
½ teaspoon vanilla essence
500 g (*1 lb*) cooking apples, peeled,
cored and chopped
65 g (*2½ oz*) chopped walnuts
125 ml (*4 fl oz*) double cream, whipped

Beat the egg with an electric mixer, then gradually add the sugar and continue beating for about 3 minutes until the sugar is dissolved and the mixture is thick and pale. Blend in the flour, baking powder and vanilla essence, then stir in the apples and walnuts.

Pour the batter into a greased 23 cm (*9 inch*) pie dish or shallow 1.2 litre (*2 pint*) baking dish. Bake in a preheated oven, 180°C (*350°F*), Gas Mark 4, for 25-30 minutes until well browned on top. Set aside and allow to cool completely.

To serve, spoon into small glass bowls, layering a little whipped cream in the middle. Top with an extra dollop of whipped cream, and serve.

APPLE ROULADE

Serves 4-6

500 g (*1 lb*) tart apples, peeled,
cored and sliced
grated rind and juice of 1 lemon
3 tablespoons icing sugar
50 g (*2 oz*) ground almonds
4 eggs, separated
250 g (*8 oz*) raspberries

Place apples in a saucepan with lemon rind, juice and 2 tablespoons of the icing sugar. Cover and cook gently for 15 minutes until soft. Purée them in a liquidizer or food processor, or rub through a sieve. Place in a bowl, stir in the ground almonds, allow to cool completely before beating the egg yolks into the apple purée. Whisk the egg whites until stiff, fold lightly into the apple purée.

Line a 32.5 x 23 cm (*13 x 9 inch*) Swiss roll tin with oiled greaseproof paper. Spread the apple mixture in the tin. Bake in a preheated oven, 200°C (*400°F*), Gas Mark 6, for 10-15 minutes, until firm and beginning to brown.

Dust a sheet of greaseproof paper with the remaining icing sugar. Turn the roulade out on to the prepared paper, peel off the baking paper. Spread the raspberries over the roulade to within 2.5 cm (*1 inch*) of the edges. Lift up the greaseproof paper to roll up the roulade. Lift carefully on to a dish, serve hot or cold.

CALVADOS APPLES

Serves 4

125 g (*4 oz*) sugar
300 ml (*½ pint*) water
6 dessert apples, peeled and quartered
3 tablespoons Calvados or brandy
brandy snaps, to serve

CARAMEL:

75 g (*3 oz*) sugar
3 tablespoons water

Place the sugar and water in a saucepan and heat gently, stirring until dissolved. Bring to the boil, then simmer for 5 minutes. Place the apples in the syrup, cover and simmer gently for 15-20 minutes until the apples look clear. Leave to cool in the syrup, then transfer the apples to a glass serving dish.

Boil the syrup rapidly until reduced by about half, then add the Calvados or brandy. Pour over the apples. Leave to cool.

To make the caramel, place the sugar and water in a pan and heat gently, stirring, until dissolved, then boil rapidly until golden brown. Pour on to an oiled baking sheet and leave to harden. When set, crack into pieces and sprinkle over the apples. Serve immediately with brandy snaps.

PLUM & APPLE MOULD

Serves 4

50 g (*2 oz*) butter
2 tablespoons cold water
250 g (*8 oz*) plums, stoned
250 g (*8 oz*) tart apples, peeled,
cored and thinly sliced
sugar, to taste
2 eggs, beaten
½ x 11 g (*0.4 oz*) sachet powdered gelatine,
soaked in 2 tablespoons cold water
150 ml (*¼ pint*) natural yogurt

Melt the butter in a large saucepan. Stir in the water and add the fruit. Simmer gently, stirring occasionally, until tender. Purée the fruit in a liquidizer or food processor, or rub through a sieve. Return the purée to the pan and add sugar to taste. Continue to cook over a low heat, stirring constantly, until the purée has thickened.

Remove the pan from the heat and stir in the eggs. Return the pan to the heat and stir constantly until the mixture thickens. Stir in the gelatine. Set aside to cool.

Stir the yogurt into the mixture. Spoon into a serving bowl or mould and chill for at least 2 hours, or until set. To serve, dip the mould or bowl into hot water for 10 seconds and then invert on to a serving plate.

TOFFEE APPLE CHEESECAKE

Serves 8-10

BASE:

75 g (*3 oz*) butter or margarine
1 tablespoon sugar
175 g (*6 oz*) oatmeal biscuit crumbs

FILLING:

500 g (*1 lb*) curd cheese
2 eggs, separated
125 g (*4 oz*) sugar
grated rind and juice of ½ lemon
11 g (*0.4 oz*) sachet powdered gelatine
75 ml (*3 fl oz*) apple juice
125 ml (*4 fl oz*) double cream, whipped
175 g (*6 oz*) unsweetened apple purée
1 teaspoon ground cinnamon

TOPPING:

65 g (*2½ oz*) sugar
3 tablespoons water
125 ml (*4 fl oz*) double cream
150 ml (*¼ pint*) whipping cream, whipped
1 apple, cored and sliced and brushed with
1 tablespoon lemon juice

Melt the butter or margarine in a saucepan. Stir in the sugar and biscuit crumbs. Press the crumb mixture on to the bottom of a greased 20 cm (*8 inch*) deep cake tin. Chill.

Beat the curd cheese in a large mixing bowl. Beat in the egg yolks, sugar and lemon rind and juice.

Sprinkle the gelatine over the apple juice in a small saucepan and let stand for 3 minutes. Place the saucepan over a low heat and heat, stirring, until the gelatine is dissolved. Beat the gelatine into the cheese mixture. Fold in the double cream, apple purée and cinnamon. Refrigerate until the mixture is almost set.

Beat the egg whites until stiff. Fold into the cheese mixture. Spoon the cheesecake mixture into the prepared tin and smooth the top. Chill for 3-4 hours or until the filling is set.

For the topping, place the sugar and water in a small saucepan and stir over a low heat until the sugar is dissolved. Bring to the boil and boil gently until the mixture is a thick golden syrup. Remove from the heat and leave for a few seconds only, to let the bubbles subside. Gradually stir in the double cream. Reheat gently to dissolve any solidified caramel. Cool.

Carefully remove the sides of the tin and place the cheesecake on a serving plate. Spread the toffee-flavoured cream on top of the cheese-cake and decorate around the edge with whipped cream and apple slices.

Illustrated opposite

APPLE NUT VACHERIN

Serves 8

MERINGUE:

4 egg whites
250 g (*8 oz*) caster sugar
125 g (*4 oz*) ground hazelnuts

FILLING:

875 g (*1¼ lb*) cooking apples, peeled,
cored and thinly sliced
125 g (*4 oz*) caster sugar
25 g (*1 oz*) butter
2 teaspoons lemon juice
300 ml (*½ pint*) whipping cream

TO DECORATE:

apple slices
toasted hazelnuts

Mark the underside of each of three sheets of non-stick silicone paper with an 18 cm (*7 inch*) circle and place each sheet on a lightly greased baking sheet.

Whisk the egg whites until stiff and gradually whisk in the caster sugar, a tablespoon at a time, continuing to whisk until thick and glossy. Lightly fold in the ground hazelnuts, using a large metal spoon. Divide the mixture between the three circles and spread out on the paper with a palette knife.

Cook in a preheated oven, 160°C (*325°F*), Gas Mark 3, for 35-40 minutes until lightly golden and crisp on the outside. Remove the meringues from the oven and leave to cool. Carefully remove from the paper.

To make the filling, put the sliced apples in a saucepan with the caster sugar, butter and lemon juice. Cover the pan and cook for 15 minutes until tender. Remove the lid and beat well with a wooden spoon then continue cooking for a further 5-8 minutes until the apples form a thick purée. Remove from the heat and leave to cool.

About 1 hour before serving, whip the cream until it forms soft peaks and fold two-thirds of the quantity into the apple purée. Place one meringue round on a serving plate and spread with half of the apple purée. Place the second round on top, spread it with the remaining purée and top with the third round.

Pipe swirls of the remaining cream on top of the meringue and decorate with the apple slices and toasted hazelnuts.

Illustrated on pages 2-3

TOFFEE APPLE ICE-CREAM

Serves 6

500 g (*1 lb*) cooking apples, peeled,
cored and roughly chopped
250 ml (*8 fl oz*) water plus 1 tablespoon
25 g (*1 oz*) butter, cut into small pieces
50 g (*2 oz*) sugar
2 egg yolks
300 ml (*½ pint*) double cream, whipped

Put apples in a saucepan with the 1 table-spoon water, cover, and heat gently until they form a purée. Beat in the butter until smooth and let cool.

Put sugar and 150 ml (*¼ pint*) of the water into a small heavy-based saucepan, stir continuously over a low heat until sugar dissolves completely. Bring to boil, then leave to bubble until a deep golden brown, remove the pan from the heat immediately. Pour on remaining water and stir until caramel dissolves. Return the pan to the heat and boil until the sauce becomes syrupy and reduces by half.

Meanwhile, beat the egg yolks in a bowl until thick and pale. Continue beating and pour on the hot caramel sauce in a thin stream, beating until cool. Fold the apple purée and whipped cream into the egg mixture, and transfer to a freezer container. Cover and freeze until firm without further beating (it may be kept frozen for up to 6 months).

BLACKBERRY & APPLE ICE-CREAM

Serves 8

1 kg (*2 lb*) cooking apples, peeled,
cored and roughly chopped
2 tablespoons lemon juice
2 tablespoons water
250 g (*8 oz*) blackberries
150 g (*5 oz*) caster sugar
300 ml (*10 fl oz*) natural yogurt, chilled
150 ml (*¼ pint*) double cream, chilled

TO DECORATE

a few blackberries
apple slices, brushed with lemon juice

Place the apples in a saucepan with the lemon juice and water, cover and cook gently until the apples soften and begin to form a purée.

Stir in the blackberries and sugar and continue to cook for about 5 minutes until the juice runs out of the blackberries. Rub the mixture through a sieve and pour into a freezer container. Refrigerate for 1 hour.

Stir the yogurt into the chilled mixture. Whip the cream until soft peaks form and fold into the mixture. Freeze until firm, beating twice at hourly intervals. (The ice-cream may be frozen for up to 6 months.) Serve in individual glass dishes and decorate with blackberries and apple slices.

APPLE & REDCURRANT SNOW

Serves 4

750 g (*1½ lb*) tart apples, peeled,
cored and sliced
4 tablespoons redcurrant jelly
2 tablespoons lemon juice
150 ml (*¼ pint*) natural yogurt
2 egg whites
40 g (*1½ oz*) caster sugar
1 tablespoon cold water
50 g (*2 oz*) flaked almonds

Place apples in a saucepan with 3 tablespoons of the redcurrant jelly and the lemon juice. Cover, cook over low heat, stirring occasionally, for 15 minutes, or until apples are soft.

Purée apples in a liquidizer or food processor, or rub through a sieve. Let the purée cool, then stir in the yogurt. Whisk the egg whites until stiff then whisk in the sugar and fold into the apple and yogurt mixture. Spoon into one serving bowl or four individual dishes.

Gently heat the remaining redcurrant jelly in a saucepan with the water until the jelly has dissolved. Add the flaked almonds to the pan. Stir gently until the almonds are glazed. Turn out on to a plate or a piece of foil and allow to cool. Arrange the glazed almonds on top of the 'snow' and serve.

APPLE SORBET

Serves 4

150 ml (*¼ pint*) dry white wine
50 g (*2 oz*) soft light brown sugar
a strip of thinly pared lemon rind
2 tablespoons lemon juice
a small piece of fresh root ginger, peeled
500 g (*1 lb*) cooking apples, peeled,
cored and sliced
2 egg whites
small herb leaves such as lemon geranium,
to decorate

Put the wine, sugar, lemon rind and juice and ginger into a saucepan and stir over a low heat until the sugar dissolves. Increase the heat and bring to the boil. Add the apple slices, poach them 8-10 minutes, or until soft. Remove from the heat and leave to cool.

Discard the lemon rind and ginger and purée the fruit in a liquidizer or food processor, or rub through a sieve. Pour into a freezer container, cover and freeze for 1 hour.

Beat the egg whites until stiff. Turn the frozen mixture into a chilled bowl and beat it to break down the ice crystals. Fold in the egg whites. Return the mixture to the freezer for 3-4 hours, until firm. To serve, transfer the sorbet to the refrigerator for 30 minutes, scoop out and decorate with the herb leaves.

Illustrated opposite

APPLE LOAF

Makes 1 small loaf

375 g (*12 oz*) plain flour
3 teaspoons baking powder
125 g (*4 oz*) butter or margarine
125 g (*4 oz*) sugar
1 teaspoon ground mixed spice
½ teaspoon ground cloves
175 g (*6 oz*) cooking apples, peeled,
cored and grated
50 ml (*2 fl oz*) medium sweet cider
1 tablespoon demerara sugar

Sift the flour into a bowl with the baking powder. Rub in the fat until the mixture resembles fine breadcrumbs. Stir in the sugar and spices, then add the apples and mix well. Stir in the cider to make a stiff mixture.

Turn the mixture into a well-greased 1 kg (*2 lb*) loaf tin. Sprinkle with the demerara sugar and bake in a preheated oven, 190°C (*375°F*), Gas Mark 5, for 50-55 minutes, or until risen, golden on top and firm to the touch. When cooked, a skewer inserted into the middle of the loaf should come out clean. Leave in the tin for a few minutes, before turning out to cool on a wire rack.

Serve warm or cold, cut into thick slices, with butter and clotted cream.

DUTCH APPLE CAKE

Makes a 20 cm (8 inch) *round cake*

275 g (*9 oz*) self-raising flour
½ teaspoon salt
1 tablespoon sugar
125 g (*4 oz*) butter
125 ml (*4 fl oz*) milk
2 Granny Smith apples, peeled,
cored and thinly sliced

TOPPING:

25 g (*1 oz*) butter, melted
1 teaspoon cinnamon
2 tablespoons sugar

Grease a 20 cm (*8 inch*) round cake tin and line the base with greaseproof paper.

Sift the flour, salt and sugar together, and rub in the butter with fingertips. Make a well in the centre and add the milk in a steady stream, stirring with a fork and incorporating the flour. Place the mixture in the prepared tin and pat level, making sure it is pushed well into the edges and against the sides.

Arrange the apples in a circular pattern to cover the top of the cake, pressing the thin edges into the dough. Brush with melted butter, sprinkle with cinnamon and sugar, and bake in a preheated oven, 180°C (*350°F*), Gas Mark 4, for 55 minutes. This cake is best served warm, cut into wedges and buttered.

CARROT & APPLE CAKE

Makes 16-20 pieces

125 g (*4 oz*) soft brown sugar
2 eggs, beaten
150 ml (*¼ pint*) sunflower oil
75 g (*3 oz*) self-raising flour
125 g (*4 oz*) plain wholemeal flour
2 teaspoons baking powder
½ teaspoon bicarbonate of soda
1 teaspoon mixed spice
½ teaspoon ground ginger
½ teaspoon grated nutmeg
175 g (*6 oz*) carrot, grated
1 dessert apple, peeled, cored and grated
50 g (*2 oz*) sultanas
1 tablespoon apple juice
75 g (*3 oz*) low-fat soft cheese
100 ml (*3½ fl oz*) natural yogurt
50 g (*2 oz*) chopped nuts

Beat together sugar and eggs until frothy. Gradually beat in the oil. Combine the dry ingredients, stir into the egg mixture with the carrot, apple and sultanas. Add apple juice to give consistency of thick batter. Pour into a greased, base-lined 18 cm (*7 inch*) square cake tin. Bake in a preheated oven, 180°C (*350°F*), Gas Mark 4, for 50-60 minutes or until firm and risen. Cool on a wire rack. Beat together the soft cheese and yogurt. Drizzle over the cake, sprinkle with nuts and cut into squares.

CHOCOLATE & APPLE CAKE

*Makes an 18 cm (*7 inch*) square cake*

125 g (*4 oz*) plain flour
1 teaspoon mixed spice
1 teaspoon baking powder
½ teaspoon bicarbonate of soda
125 g (*4 oz*) plain wholemeal flour
125 g (*4 oz*) butter or hard margarine
175 g (*6 oz*) light soft brown sugar
2 eggs (size 2), beaten
125 g (*4 oz*) currants
125 g (*4 oz*) raisins or sultanas
75 g (*3 oz*) chocolate dots (plain or milk)
grated rind of 1 small orange
125 g (*4 oz*) peeled cooking apple, coarsely grated
2 tablespoons demerara sugar

Sift plain flour, spice, baking powder and soda into a bowl, add wholemeal flour. Cream fat and sugar in a bowl until pale and fluffy. Add eggs, one at a time, adding a little flour after each. Fold in remaining flour then the rest of the ingredients except the demerara. Add 1 tablespoon water if the mixture seems too dry. Turn into a greased and lined 18 cm (*7 inch*) square cake tin. Level, sprinkle with demerara. Bake in a preheated oven, 180°C (*350°F*), Gas Mark 4, for about 1¼ hours or until firm to the touch and golden brown. Cool in the tin for 5 minutes then turn out on to a wire tray. Store in an airtight container when cold – best left 48 hours before cutting.

APPLESAUCE CAKE

Makes 9 squares

150 g (*5 oz*) raisins
250 g (*8 oz*) plain flour
2 teaspoons bicarbonate of soda
½ teaspoon grated nutmeg
¼ teaspoon ground cloves
½ teaspoon ground cinnamon
125 g (*4 oz*) butter
175 g (*6 oz*) light brown sugar
1 egg
½ teaspoon vanilla essence
350 g (*11½ oz*) unsweetened apple purée
125 g (*4 oz*) walnuts or pecans, chopped
to decorate (optional)
chopped walnuts or pecans,

ICING:

250 g (*8 oz*) cream cheese
40 g (*1½ oz*) dark brown sugar
¼ teaspoon grated orange rind
¼ teaspoon vanilla essence
2 teaspoons single cream or milk

Soak the raisins in enough hot water to cover them for 15 minutes, then drain, discarding the soaking water.

Sift the plain flour, bicarbonate of soda and spices together and set aside.

Beat the butter with the brown sugar until well creamed and the sugar has dissolved.

Beat in the egg and vanilla essence, then stir in the apple purée and chopped nuts. Add the dry ingredients to the creamed mixture in three batches, folding well to combine after each addition.

Pour into a well-greased 23 cm (*9 inch*) square, or 19 x 28 cm (*7½ x 11 inch*) rectangular, baking tin. Bake in a preheated oven, 180°C (*350°F*), Gas Mark 4, for about 50 minutes, or until a skewer inserted in the centre comes out clean. Cool in the baking tin on a wire rack.

Beat all the icing ingredients together until smooth and well blended. Spread the icing over the top of the cooled cake. Decorate with chopped walnuts or pecans, if desired. Cut into squares to serve.

Illustrated opposite

APPLE CHEESE CAKES

Makes 12

250 g (*8 oz*) apples, cored and roughly
chopped (not peeled)
4-5 tablespoons water
thinly pared rind of ½ lemon
2-3 whole cloves
½ stick cinnamon,
or pinch of ground cinnamon
1-2 tablespoons sugar
25 g (*1 oz*) butter
scant 25 g (*1 oz*) cake crumbs or fresh
breadcrumbs
2 egg yolks, or 1 whole egg, beaten
caster sugar, for sprinkling

PASTRY:

125 g (*4 oz*) plain flour
pinch of salt
50 g (*2 oz*) butter
15 g (*½ oz*) caster sugar
1 egg yolk

To make the pastry, sift the plain flour and
salt into a mixing bowl. Cut the butter into
the flour and rub in until the mixture
resembles breadcrumbs. Stir in the caster
sugar, then stir in the egg yolk to bind to a
firm dough, adding a little cold water if
necessary.

Knead lightly until smooth but do not
overwork the pastry. Leave to rest in the
refrigerator or a cool place for at least
30 minutes before rolling out.

Place the apples, water, lemon rind, cloves,
cinnamon and sugar in a saucepan. Cover and
cook until softened. Remove the lid and
continue cooking into a thick pulp, stirring
frequently so it does not stick. Remove the
cinnamon stick, if using.

Purée the apples in a liquidizer or food
processor, or rub through a sieve, and return
to the rinsed pan over a gentle heat. Add the
butter and when melted remove the pan from
the heat. Cool slightly, then stir in the cake
crumbs or fresh breadcrumbs and egg. Leave
until cold.

Roll out the pastry thinly and line 12 patty
tins. Prick the bottom of each and three-
quarters fill with the apple mixture. Bake in a
preheated oven, 200°C (*400°F*), Gas Mark 6,
for 20 minutes, or until the pastry is crisp and
the filling set. Remove from the tins and cool
on a wire tray. When cold, sprinkle generously
with caster sugar, and serve.

LITTLE MARZIPAN & APPLE PIES

Makes 12

milk, for brushing
1 tablespoon demerara sugar (optional)

FILLING:

200 g (*7 oz*) cooking apples, peeled,
cored and coarsely chopped
75 g (*3 oz*) ready-made marzipan,
cut into 5 mm (*¼ inch*) cubes

PASTRY:

125 g (*4 oz*) plain flour
125 g (*4 oz*) wholemeal flour
pinch of salt
125 g (*4 oz*) hard vegetable margarine,
from the freezer
3-4 tablespoons water

To make the pastry, put both the flours and salt into a large bowl. Grate the hard margarine straight into the flours, dipping it into the bowl now and again to free the flakes of margarine. Distribute the margarine gently through the flour, using a round-bladed knife, then add the water as necessary. Mix to a fairly firm dough then put the pastry into a polythene bag and chill in the refrigerator for 1 hour if possible.

For the filling, mix the chopped apple and marzipan cubes together in a bowl.

Roll out the pastry quite thinly on a lightly floured surface. Cut out twelve rounds using a 7 cm (*3 inch*) fluted cutter, and twelve rounds using a 5 cm (*2 inch*) fluted cutter. Line twelve small tartlet tins with the larger rounds and spoon the apple and marzipan filling into them, packing it in well.

Brush both sides of the remaining rounds with milk and lay them on top of the tartlets in the tin. Press the edges together to seal and sprinkle each one with a little demerara sugar, if liked.

Bake near the top of a preheated oven, 220°C (*425°F*), Gas Mark 7, for 15-20 minutes until golden brown. Remove carefully from the tins and leave to cool slightly on a wire tray. Serve warm or cold.

DATE & APPLE CRUNCHIES

Makes 16

125 g (*4 oz*) butter or margarine
125 g (*4 oz*) soft brown sugar
3 tablespoons golden syrup
175 g (*6 oz*) rolled oats
50 g (*2 oz*) wholemeal flour
1 teaspoon baking powder
125 g (*4 oz*) stoned dates, chopped
250 g (*8 oz*) apples, peeled,
cored and finely chopped

Melt the fat with the sugar and golden syrup in a saucepan over a gentle heat. Stir well and do not allow to boil. Set aside to cool. Mix together the rolled oats, flour and baking powder. Stir in the cooled liquid ingredients and mix very thoroughly.

Turn half the mixture into a greased 18 cm (*7 inch*) square tin, spread out evenly and press down with a wooden spoon. Mix the chopped dates with the apples and spread over the oat mixture. Cover with the remaining mixture and press down firmly.

Bake in a preheated oven, 180°C (*350°F*), Gas Mark 4, for 30-35 minutes until firm and golden. Remove from oven, cut into squares. Allow to cool, remove from the tin and cool on a wire tray. Store in an airtight container.

HOT APPLE MUFFINS

Makes 24

250 g (*8 oz*) plain flour
1 teaspoon salt
3 teaspoons baking powder
50 g (*2 oz*) caster sugar
½ teaspoon ground ginger
½ teaspoon mixed spice
2 eggs, beaten
150 ml (*¼ pint*) milk
50 g (*2 oz*) butter, melted
250 g (*8 oz*) cooking or dessert apples,
peeled, cored and finely chopped

Grease 24 x 5 cm (*2 inch*) muffin or bun tins. Sift the flour, salt and baking powder into a mixing bowl. Stir in the sugar and spices. In a small bowl beat the eggs with the milk and mix in the melted butter. Stir the liquid quickly into the flour mixture. Speed is essential once the liquid is added to the baking powder, so do not beat the mixture or bother about any lumps. Fold in the chopped apples. Spoon the mixture into the greased bun tins so they are one-third full.

Bake in a preheated oven, 220°C (*425°F*), Gas Mark 7, for 15-20 minutes or until well risen and golden brown. Turn out of the tins and serve hot, split and buttered.

Illustrated opposite

SPICED APPLE DRINK

Makes 2.4 litres (4 pints)

500 g (*1 lb*) apples
2.4 litres (*4 pints*) cold water
250 g (*8 oz*) sugar
1 tablespoon ground ginger
1 tablespoon ground cinnamon
½ tablespoon whole cloves
½ tablespoon allspice

Wash the apples and grate them coarsely into a clean 2.4 litre (*4 pint*) wide-necked container, such as a plastic bucket or bowl. Add the cores and cold water. Put in a cool place for 1 week and stir once a day.

Add the sugar and spices. Stir the liquid until the sugar has dissolved. Leave to stand for 1 day more, then strain the liquid through a muslin cloth. Syphon or pour the liquid into clean bottles.

Lightly cork the bottles and leave them in a cool place for 1 week before drinking.

MULLED APPLE JUICE

Makes 900 ml (1½ pints)

500 g (*1 lb*) cooking apples, peeled,
cored and sliced
600 ml (*1 pint*) water
finely grated rind and juice of 2 oranges
6 tablespoons clear honey
6 whole cloves, or large pinch of ground cloves
1 cinnamon stick, or pinch of ground cinnamon
1 teaspoon grated nutmeg
pinch of ground ginger
2 tablespoons rum or brandy

TO DECORATE:

whole cloves
apple slices

Put all of the ingredients, except the rum or brandy, in a saucepan. Bring to the boil, then lower the heat, cover the pan and simmer for about 10 minutes until the apples are reduced to a pulp.

Transfer to a liquidizer or food processor and blend until the apples are smooth, but the whole spices, if used, are still in pieces.

Strain the juice, stir in the rum or brandy and serve hot, decorated with whole cloves and slices of apple.

Illustrated on pages 2-3

BRAMBLE & APPLE JAM

Makes about 3.5 kg (7 lb)

**1 kg (*2 lb*) cooking apples, peeled, cored
and sliced with trimmings reserved
300 ml (*½ pint*) water
1 kg (*2 lb*) blackberries
2 kg (*4 lb*) preserving sugar
8 tablespoons lemon juice**

Boil apple trimmings in a saucepan with the water for 15 minutes, or until most of water has evaporated. Put apples, blackberries and 250 g (*8 oz*) of the sugar in a large pan. Press apple trimmings through fine sieve to extract the pulp and pectin, add this to the fruit. Heat gently until juice runs from blackberries, cook for 5-10 minutes, or until apples are soft.

Add remaining sugar to pan, stir over a gentle heat until completely dissolved. Add lemon juice. Bring to the boil, boiling hard until setting point is reached: put a little jam on a very cold saucer and let cool. As it cools, if the setting point is reached a skin will form on the surface and will wrinkle when the jam is gently pushed with one finger. Alternatively, use a sugar thermometer – this should register 104°C (*220°F*) when setting point is reached.

Have ready warmed pots. Pour in the hot jam, cover with waxed discs, waxed sides down. Cool. Cover pots with cellophane tops or air-tight lids and store, unopened, for 6-9 months.

APPLE MINCEMEAT

*Makes about 3 kg (*6 lb*)*

**500 g (*1 lb*) cooking apples, peeled,
cored and grated
250 g (*8 oz*) cut mixed peel
500 g (*1 lb*) currants
500 g (*1 lb*) sultanas
500 g (*1 lb*) raisins
175 g (*6 oz*) shredded suet or
chilled butter, grated
500 g (*1 lb*) granulated or soft brown sugar
125 g (*4 oz*) almonds, skinned and chopped
1½ teaspoons ground mixed spice
1 teaspoon grated nutmeg
grated rind and juice of 1 lemon
150 ml (*¼ pint*) brandy or rum**

Place all of the ingredients, except the brandy or rum, in a large bowl and mix well. Cover and leave for 24 hours, then add the spirit and mix again. Pack the mincemeat into sterilized jars and cover.

If the mincemeat is to be kept for more than a few weeks, seal the jars with an airtight cover – glass or plastic-coated lids are suitable, or corks which have been soaked in boiling water for 15 minutes to sterilize them.

APPLE & HORSERADISH SAUCE

Makes about 450 ml (¾ pint)

500 g (*1 lb*) cooking apples, roughly chopped
2 tablespoons water
2 whole cloves
50 g (*2 oz*) sugar
25 g (*1 oz*) butter
1 teaspoon lemon juice
2 tablespoons grated horseradish
or bottled horseradish sauce

Place the chopped apples in a saucepan with the water, cloves and sugar. Simmer until tender, then beat until smooth. Purée in a liquidizer or food processor, or rub through a sieve. Stir in the butter, lemon juice and horseradish and reheat gently. Serve the sauce with a variety of fish or meat.

APPLE CHUTNEY

Makes about 3 kg (6 lb)

1.5 kg (*3 lb*) cooking apples, peeled, cored and chopped
1.5 kg (*3 lb*) onions, chopped
375 g (*12 oz*) raisins
50 g (*2 oz*) fresh root ginger, grated
1 green pepper, seeded and chopped
1 tablespoon mustard powder
1 tablespoon ground coriander
3 garlic cloves, crushed
750 g (*1½ lb*) demerara sugar
600 ml (*1 pint*) vinegar

Put all the ingredients together in a large saucepan and mix well. Bring slowly to the boil, stirring occasionally, then reduce the heat and cover the pan. Leave the chutney to simmer for about 2 hours, or until the mixture is of a thick consistency. Stir the mixture often to prevent it sticking to the pan.

Have ready clean, warmed pots. Spoon the chutney into the pots and cover with waxed discs, waxed sides down. Top immediately with airtight lids. Store for a few weeks before sampling, the chutney can then be kept for up to 6 months.

Illustrated opposite

APPLE SAUCE

Makes about 350 ml (12 fl oz)
50 g (*2 oz*) butter
1 large Spanish onion, finely diced
8 fresh sage leaves, chopped,
or 2 teaspoons dried
2 tablespoons demerara sugar
500 g (*1 lb*) dessert apples, peeled,
cored and sliced
salt and freshly ground black pepper

Melt the butter in a saucepan and gently fry the onion. Add the sage and salt and pepper, and cook until the onion is soft and transparent, stirring occasionally.

Sprinkle over the demerara sugar, increase the heat and stir in the sliced apples. Cook for 7-10 minutes, turning the mixture over occasionally with a wooden spoon, but taking care not to break the apple slices.

As soon as the apples are soft, but not mushy, remove from the heat. The sauce makes an ideal accompaniment to serve with duck, pork or goose.

SPICED APPLE SLICES

Makes about 2 kg (4 lb)
500 g (*1 lb*) sugar
600 ml·(*1 pint*) white vinegar
1 teaspoon salt
125 ml (*4 fl oz*) water
15 cm (*6 inch*) stick cinnamon
2 teaspoons whole cloves
few drops red food colouring
1.5 kg (*3 lb*) dessert apples, peeled,
cored and thickly sliced

Put the sugar and white vinegar into a saucepan with the salt and water. Tie the spices in a piece of muslin and hang them in the pan. Stir over a low heat until the sugar has dissolved. Add a little food colouring and stir to colour evenly.

Drop the apple slices into the hot spiced syrup and cook gently until the slices are tender but still keep their shape. Skim out the slices and pack them into warm preserving jars. Then heat the syrup to boiling point and pour into the jars, covering the apple slices. Cover tightly.

These are delicious served with cold lamb, ham and pork, or with cold goose or duck.

APPLE & APRICOT STUFFING

Makes enough to stuff a 1.5 kg (3lb) chicken

**1 large cooking apple, peeled,
cored and finely chopped
125 g (*4 oz*) dried apricots, chopped
125 g (*4 oz*) fresh breadcrumbs
1 onion, finely chopped
1 teaspoon dried thyme
1 teaspoon dried sage
4 tablespoons brandy or dry sherry
2 tablespoons orange juice
salt and freshly ground black pepper**

Mix the chopped apple and apricots with the fresh breadcrumbs. Add the chopped onion, dried herbs, brandy or dry sherry and orange juice. Season and mix well to make a moist stuffing for roast chicken.

APPLE & RAISIN STUFFING

Makes enough to stuff a 1.5 kg (3lb) chicken

**50 g (*2 oz*) butter
1 onion, finely chopped
8 fresh sage leaves, chopped,
or 2 teaspoons dried
250 g (*8 oz*) dessert apples, peeled,
cored and diced
40 g (*1½ oz*) long-grain rice, cooked
and drained
50 g (*2 oz*) raisins
1 egg yolk, lightly beaten
salt and freshly ground black pepper**

Melt the butter in a saucepan and gently fry the onion for 4 minutes, until soft and transparent. Increase the heat, add the sage and diced apples, and toss over the heat for 6-7 minutes, until the apples soften but do not entirely lose their shape.

Add the rice, raisins and salt and pepper, stirring well. Remove from the heat and cool slightly. Beat in the egg yolk to bind all the ingredients together. Use for stuffing a roast chicken or serve with duck, goose or pork.

—THE—
APPLE
INDEX